THE
MUCKRAKERS

IDA TARBELL TAKES ON
BIG BUSINESS

BY VALERIE BODDEN

CONTENT CONSULTANT
STEVE WEINBERG
AUTHOR
*TAKING ON THE TRUST: THE EPIC BATTLE OF
IDA TARBELL AND JOHN D. ROCKEFELLER*

Essential Library

An Imprint of Abdo Publishing | abdopublishing.com

ABDOPUBLISHING.COM

Published by Abdo Publishing, a division of ABDO, PO Box 398166, Minneapolis, Minnesota 55439. Copyright © 2017 by Abdo Consulting Group, Inc. International copyrights reserved in all countries. No part of this book may be reproduced in any form without written permission from the publisher. Essential Library™ is a trademark and logo of Abdo Publishing.

Printed in the United States of America, North Mankato, Minnesota
102016
012017

THIS BOOK CONTAINS
RECYCLED MATERIALS

Cover Photo: Bettmann/Getty Images
Interior Photos: J. E. Purdy/Library of Congress, 4–5; Library of Congress, 11, 18, 22, 47, 74; North Wind Picture Archives, 12–13, 36–37; Jacob A. Riis/Getty Images, 20; Frances Benjamin Johnston/Library of Congress, 24–25; Bettmann/Getty Images, 30, 35, 48–49, 53; Public Domain, 33; Culture Club/Getty Images, 42; Udo J. Keppler/Library of Congress, 44; Red Line Editorial, 55; MPI/Getty Images, 57; Pach Brothers/Library of Congress, 60–61; Carl Hassman/Library of Congress, 66; AP Images, 69, 78–79; G. C. Cox/Library of Congress, 70–71; John Springer Collection/Corbis/Getty Images, 82; Andrew Harrer/Bloomberg/Getty Images, 86–87; Simon Allison/AP Images, 92; Shutterstock Images, 96

Editor: Rebecca Rowell
Series Designer: Maggie Villaume

PUBLISHER'S CATALOGING-IN-PUBLICATION DATA

Names: Bodden, Valerie, author.
Title: The Muckrakers: Ida Tarbell takes on big business / by Valerie Bodden.
Other titles: Ida Tarbell takes on big business
Description: Minneapolis, MN : Abdo Publishing, 2017. | Series: Hidden heroes | Includes bibliographical references and index.
Identifiers: LCCN 2016945476 | ISBN 9781680783889 (lib. bdg.) | ISBN 9781680797411 (ebook)
Subjects: LCSH: Women journalists--United States--Juvenile literature. | Journalists--United States--Juvenile literature. | Investigative reporting--United States--Juvenile literature.
Classification: DDC 070--dc23
LC record available at http://lccn.loc.gov/2016945476

CONTENTS

CHAPTER ONE

SEEDS OF CONFLICT

Everyone told Ida Tarbell she should be scared. In 1901, the 44-year-old reporter began researching a series of articles about one of the nation's industrial giants: Standard Oil Trust. Even her father told her not to do it, saying Standard Oil had the power to ruin *McClure's*, the national magazine she worked for. But Tarbell was not afraid. Reflecting on that period of her life and the magazine years later, she wrote in her autobiography, "Courage implies a suspicion of danger. Nobody thought of such a thing in our office. We were undertaking what we regarded as a legitimate piece of historical work. . . . What had we to be afraid of?"[1]

Ida Tarbell followed her heart and conscience in exposing the shady business practices of Standard Oil.

So Tarbell began her research by digging through thousands of pages of documents and conducting dozens of interviews. Her series, the History of the Standard Oil Company, exposed the illegal and unethical practices Standard Oil had employed to take over the oil industry. People across the United States clamored to read the articles, which were so popular the original plan for a three-part series was expanded to 19 articles.

In the end, Standard Oil did not ruin *McClure's*. In fact, the magazine's circulation soared to nearly 500,000 subscribers.[2] For her part, Tarbell became one of the most famous journalists in the country.

But for Tarbell, writing the series was not about finding fame. It was about exploring and exposing a company and an industry that had been part of her life almost from the time she was born.

> "(*The History of the Standard Oil Company*) remains one of the great case studies of what a single journalist, armed with the facts, can do against seeming invincible powers."[3]
>
> —*Ron Chernow, Rockefeller biographer, 1998*

Childhood among Oil Fields

Ida Tarbell was born on November 5, 1857, in the small settlement of Hatch Hollow, Pennsylvania. Her parents, Franklin and Esther Tarbell, planned to move with their baby girl to Iowa in search of new opportunities. But before they did so, opportunity arose closer to home. In 1859, a well struck oil in northwestern Pennsylvania. It was the first successful oil well in the nation's history, and enterprising men flocked to the region to be part of the oil rush.

The automobile had not yet been invented, but oil was still a valuable commodity. It could be refined to make kerosene to fuel lamps. Before this time, lamps were generally fueled by whale oil or kerosene made from coal tar. But whale oil was in short supply, and both it and kerosene from coal were too expensive for most people to afford. The discovery of large quantities of oil meant a new, cheaper source of lamp oil would be readily available. And those who sold it could become wealthy.

Franklin Tarbell wanted to cash in on the oil boom. According to Ida, her father realized the oil business

REFINING OIL

With the discovery of oil, refineries sprang up in Pittsburgh, Pennsylvania, New York, New York, and Cleveland, Ohio. The process of refining oil began as the product was strained and loaded into wooden tanks. Next, the oil was boiled, which caused it to vaporize. The various vapors were treated in different ways to form different products. The lightest vapors formed gasoline. Other vapors became different chemical products. In the early days of the oil boom—before the invention of automobiles— kerosene was the most valuable by-product of oil because of its widespread use as a lamp fuel.

had "more money in it than he had ever dreamed of making."[4] He did not plan to drill a well himself. Rather, he would profit from building tanks in which well owners could store the oil gushing up from the ground. In 1860, he moved his family to the northwestern Pennsylvania settlement of Rouseville.

Business was soon booming, but young Ida hated her surroundings, which consisted largely of oil derricks and sunken pits where unproductive wells had been abandoned. As she later wrote,

> No industry of man in its early days has ever been more destructive of beauty, order, decency, than the production of petroleum. . . . If oil was found, if the well flowed, every tree, every shrub, every bit of grass in the vicinity was coated with black grease and left to die.[5]

Despite the ugly landscape, Ida's family continued prospering. Soon, they were able to move into a home on a hill above the town, where the view was a wooded hillside, not oil derricks. Ida enjoyed exploring these woods until 1870, when her family moved to the nearby town of Titusville. Eventually, as iron tanks replaced the wooden ones Franklin made, he turned to the wells and became an oil producer.

Invasion of the Octopus

Meanwhile, as Ida grew up in oil country, John D. Rockefeller set his eyes on the area as well. In the 1860s, the young man established a refinery in his hometown of Cleveland, Ohio. His business started out small, but Rockefeller wanted to be the biggest and the best. His company began forcing smaller oil refiners and producers to sell their companies to him. Rockefeller then incorporated their refineries and wells into his business, which eventually took the name Standard Oil Company. As the company grew and spread, some people called it the Octopus because it seemed to reach everywhere.

In 1871, Rockefeller and a few other large refiners made a secret, illegal deal with the railroads, forming a company known as the South Improvement Company to carry out the deal. The railroads

BUSINESS TYCOON

John D. Rockefeller was born on July 8, 1839, in Richford, New York. His family moved several times before finally settling permanently in Cleveland. Rockefeller's father was a con man who scammed money with schemes such as pretending to be a beggar who was deaf and unable to speak. In 1855, Rockefeller took a job as a bookkeeper. In 1859, he set up a small business selling grain, meat, and other commodities, before turning his attention to oil. His oil business eventually made Rockefeller the richest man in America. He earned $10 million to $20 million a year at a time when the average American made $500 a year.[6]

agreed to charge refiners who were part of the South Improvement Company reduced rates for shipping their oil. At the same time, the railroads would raise the rates of all other companies shipping oil. The members of the South Improvement Company would receive rebates, or money back, not only on their own shipments but also on the shipments of their competitors.

When word of the rate hikes got out, Titusville's 3,000 angry oilmen swarmed the local opera house.[7] There, they held nightly protests. Ida later remembered the excitement of those nights as her father and the other men of the town signed a pledge not to sell to Standard Oil. In what became known as the Oil War of 1872, angry mobs went so far as to destroy the tank cars of oil producers who gave in to Rockefeller.

Crusader of the Future

The railroad rebate scheme was eventually canceled, but Ida later remembered the Oil War of 1872 as the start of her "hatred of privilege—privilege of any sort."[8] It was the first time she realized it was every individual's "duty to fight injustice."[9] She had no way of knowing this was only the start of her fight against injustice.

Nearly 30 years later, that fight would bring her into conflict with Rockefeller again. This time, it would take place in one of the nation's most popular magazines,

John D. Rockefeller made millions of dollars in the oil business and controlled the industry.

with Ida as the star reporter. And, in the end, the clash would change the course of US business and the role of journalism in American life.

CHAPTER TWO

KEEPING THE PEOPLE INFORMED

Journalism already had a long history in the United States by the time Tarbell was born. Almost from the time settlers began arriving in North America, newspapers had been distributed to keep citizens informed. Many of these early papers were strongly partisan, openly supporting various political candidates. Others were published by religious groups or other organizations interested in promoting a specific cause. Most early papers cost approximately $6 to $10 per year and had to be paid for in advance.[1] This was more than the average family could afford.

An 1883 ad promoted the *New York Sun*, which cost $6.50 a year for a daily subscription.

By the early 1800s, printing and paper production costs had gone down, leading to the establishment of the penny press. As the name suggests, penny press newspapers were sold for one cent an issue. They did not have to be paid for in advance but could be bought from street vendors each day. The first American paper to be sold for a penny was the *New York Sun*, established by Benjamin Day in 1833. With easy-to-read, entertaining stories—many of them loosely based on fact or even completely made up—the *Sun* soon had a circulation of 130,000.[2]

Other newspapers of the time established more rigorous journalistic standards. Some helped expose corruption and scandal, publishing some of the first investigative pieces. An 1858 article in *Frank Leslie's Illustrated*

ENTERTAINMENT VERSUS FACT

In the early days of the penny press, entertainment was often valued over fact. In 1835, the *New York Sun* ran a series of articles about the discovery of life on the moon. Reporter Richard Adams Locke claimed a British astronomer had observed living creatures on the moon. According to the article, the creatures "averaged four feet (1.2 m) in height, were covered, except on the face, with short and glossy copper-colored hair, and had wings composed of a thin membrane."[3] Publication of the story led the *Sun's* circulation to more than double. But when scientists from Yale University asked to see the reports, it quickly became clear the story was a hoax. Locke had made everything up. Readers did not seem to mind.

Newspaper, for example, revealed that local New York dairies were selling swill milk from cows fed on waste products from nearby distilleries producing whiskey. The milk had been doctored with plaster of paris, a white, powdery substance used to make casts and molds, to make it look normal. The tainted milk caused the deaths of thousands of infants. Leslie published the names of those delivering the swill milk. Within a week, all had gone out of business. The increased attention on the issue also helped bring about a state law banning the sale of swill milk.

Yellow Journalism

By the late 1800s, reports of scandal and corruption were becoming more popular in newspapers across the country. In 1883, Joseph Pulitzer, who had previously served as editor and publisher of the

JOSEPH PULITZER

Born in Hungary on April 10, 1847, Joseph Pulitzer immigrated to the United States in 1864. After fighting in the American Civil War (1861–1865) on the side of the Union, Pulitzer began writing for a German-language newspaper. In 1878, he purchased the *Dispatch* and *Post* newspapers in Saint Louis, Missouri, and merged them into the *Saint Louis Post-Dispatch*. In 1883, he purchased the *New York World*, a paper in New York City. At his death in 1911, Pulitzer left an endowment to establish the Columbia University School of Journalism and the Pulitzer Prize, the most distinguished award in journalism. Today, Pulitzer Prizes are awarded for 21 categories in journalism and the arts each year. The awards recognize outstanding public service and achievement.

Saint Louis Post-Dispatch, purchased the *New York World*. He said the newspaper's goal was to "expose all fraud and sham, fight all public evils and abuses . . . and battle for the people with earnest sincerity."[4]

As part of this effort, Pulitzer hired Elizabeth Cochrane—who wrote under the name Nellie Bly—to serve as an undercover reporter. In 1887, Bly pretended to be insane in order to have herself committed to an insane asylum in New York. Afterward, she published an article describing conditions in the institution. Bly and other journalists like her came to be known as "stunt journalists" or "sob sisters" for the sensational stunts they pulled to make news.[5]

Bly's stories drove newspaper sales, and by 1895, the *World* had the largest circulation in the United States. But that year, a new competitor entered the scene when William Randolph Hearst purchased the *New York Morning Journal*. The wealthy Hearst was determined to make his paper the most widely read in the country. Soon, the *World* and the *Morning Journal* were engulfed in a circulation war. Both papers concentrated their coverage on crime, scandals, and sensational stories to drive readership and sell the most papers.

Hearst lowered the price of the *Morning Journal* from two cents to one cent an issue, making it cheaper than the two-cent *World*. Hearst also hired several of the best writers, editors, and artists away from the *World* by offering them huge pay increases over what Pulitzer could give them. Among those who left the *World* to join the ranks of Hearst's staff at the *Morning Journal* was R. F. Outcault, an artist who drew the enormously popular *Hogan's Alley*, the first color comic in an American paper. More popularly known as the "Yellow Kid" because its main character was a kid wearing a yellow shirt, the comic portrayed life in the New York tenements. After

MAKING NEWS

Nellie Bly may be a better known stunt journalist, but she was not the first stunt journalist. In 1869, the *New York Herald* pulled its own stunt by sending reporter Henry Morton Stanley to Africa in search of David Livingstone. Livingstone was a Scottish explorer and missionary who had traveled to Central Africa three years earlier but was presumed lost. In November 1871, Stanley reached Livingstone, uttering words that have since become famous: "Doctor Livingstone, I presume."[7] Stanley's so-called discovery of Livingstone—who had not been lost but had chosen to remain in Africa—drove newspaper sales and made the reporter a celebrity.

An artist captured the reception Nellie Bly received in Jersey City, New Jersey, after her return from a whirlwind global adventure.

losing his artist to Hearst, Pulitzer hired artist George Luks to produce a "Yellow Kid" comic for the *World*.

With the two papers each producing their own version of the Yellow Kid, the term *yellow journalism* was coined to describe the type of sensational journalism both papers used to drive sales. Realizing yellow journalism sold papers, other newspapers turned to this style as well. Over time, many of them—including the *World*—pulled back from sensationalistic coverage. Hearst, however, kept his papers on the track of yellow journalism, eventually creating the country's largest newspaper chain.

Exposing Inequality

As the *World* and the *Morning Journal* engaged in their circulation war, other writers began covering more serious subjects, setting the stage for later investigative journalists, such as Tarbell. Danish immigrant Jacob Riis had come to America in 1870. He was 21 years old. At first, he struggled to find a job and experienced poverty firsthand. Later, as a police reporter for the *New York Tribune*, Riis spent his nights covering crime in some of the poorest neighborhoods of New York City. There, he found immigrants crammed into overcrowded, unsanitary tenement houses. Often, dozens of people lived in a single, windowless room, with no access to air or light. Others had no home and slept on the streets. Riis was deeply affected by what he saw, writing, "The sights I saw there gripped my heart until I felt that I must tell of them, or burst, or turn anarchist, or something."[8]

So Riis began writing newspaper articles exposing conditions in the slums. He called out negligent landlords who profited from the suffering of tenement residents. He also began carrying a camera with him, capturing the horrors of the slums in photographs. In 1890, Riis published *How the Other Half Lives*, a book of photographs and essays describing life in New York's urban slums. He believed seeing how the poor lived would inspire middle- and upper-class Americans to help. And he, like Tarbell and many of the investigative journalists who would follow him, asked readers, "What are you going to do about it?"[9]

Jacob Riis relied on images as well as words to tell his stories, including this photograph showing readers the poverty on New York City's East Side, where three homeless boys sought warmth on a vent.

Meanwhile, in the southern United States, African-American journalist Ida B. Wells was well-acquainted with inequality. Born into slavery in 1862, Wells gained freedom when the Civil War (1861–1865) ended. She went on to become a teacher in Tennessee. In that role, she began writing articles for the black-owned *Evening Star* in Memphis and, later, for the *Memphis Free Speech and Headlight*, where she became a part owner. Wells's articles focused on the inequalities between the education of blacks and of whites. When her controversial articles got her fired from her teaching position, Wells turned to writing full time. Her writing style was simple and easy to read. As she later explained, "I wrote in a plain, common-sense way on the things which concerned our people. Knowing that their education was limited, I never used a word of two syllables where one would serve the purpose."[10]

Wells's articles focused especially on the topic of lynching, which she said was "an excuse to get rid of Negroes who were acquiring wealth and property and thus keep the [black] race terrorized."[11] On May 21, 1892, she published an editorial calling attention to the lynching of eight black men. Five of the men had been killed for supposedly raping white women. Wells challenged that charge, writing, "Nobody . . . believes the old thread bare

Ida B. Wells used her writing to challenge social norms and received death threats as a result.

lie that Negro men rape white women" and implied that the sex had been consensual.[12]

Wells was on vacation when the article went to print. Local white citizens destroyed the newspaper office and made death threats against her. Taking the advice of friends, Wells did not return home but, instead, accepted a position with the *New York Age*. There, she continued to write about lynching, and her articles inspired the formation of several anti-lynching organizations.

Magazine Age

As newspaper circulation soared, the number of magazines being published also increased. Magazines offered a format for longer, more in-depth articles than newspapers. But until the 1880s, they were intended almost exclusively for upper-class readers. One reason was that members of the upper class were the most likely to be literate. Another was that most magazines were too expensive for the average American to afford. The best magazines, such as *Harper's Weekly* and *Century*, cost thirty-five cents per issue.

But as printing costs came down, magazines could lower their prices, allowing middle-class readers to purchase them. Rising literacy rates also created a wider audience for magazine readership. By 1890, more than 85 percent of the population could read at a basic level.[13] Publishers responded by flooding the market with periodicals. By 1900, more than 5,000 magazines were published in the United States.[14] Many were restricted to specific regions or covered special activities and hobbies. But general-interest magazines with a national circulation were also starting up. The contents of these magazines generally consisted of in-depth feature articles about current events and scientific discoveries, along with popular fiction and poetry. Although most were not originally established as forums for exposing scandal and corruption, a new type of journalism would soon develop in their pages, thanks to a new generation of reform-minded journalists, including Tarbell.

CHAPTER THREE

A MAGAZINE FOR EVERYONE

Initially, Ida Tarbell was interested in science. She had little interest in school but eventually became a model student. By the time she entered high school, Ida had decided she would never marry or have children. She wanted to be free to follow her own ambitions, which was almost impossible for a married woman.

Although few women pursued higher education, after graduating from high school, Ida enrolled in Allegheny College in Meadville, Pennsylvania. She was the only woman in her class. In addition to studying science, literature, history, economics, and art criticism, Ida joined the student newspaper.

Tarbell's decision to pursue journalism changed the field.

After graduating from Allegheny in 1880, Ida took a position as a teacher at a private school in Poland, Ohio. There, she taught French, Latin, Greek, and German, along with geology, botany, math, and English grammar. In her spare time, Ida explored her surroundings, which were being taken over by coal mines and iron mills. She witnessed the poor working conditions and slum housing of mine and factory workers and came face-to-face with men who had been burned by molten metal when a factory furnace burst.

Becoming a Writer

After two years of teaching, 24-year-old Tarbell was exhausted and ready for a change. She returned to her parents' home in Titusville. She studied with her microscope and helped around the house. Then, in 1883, a family friend, the Reverend Theodore Flood, visited. Flood was the editor of a journal called the *Chautauquan*, which published articles about everything from art, literature, science, technology, and foreign affairs to manners and hygiene. Many articles included terms and concepts that might be unfamiliar to readers, so Flood asked Tarbell if she would like to annotate the magazine, adding notes to explain anything readers might not understand on their own. Tarbell accepted the job and moved back to Meadville, where the publication's offices were located.

Soon, Tarbell was also reworking the layout and editing articles. She began writing for the magazine, too. The first article to feature her byline was "The Arts and Industries of Cincinnati." While the piece praised that city's cultural life, it also contended, "Morally, Cincinnati has much to learn."[1] While working for the *Chautauquan*, Tarbell edited numerous articles about controversial topics, including women's rights. At the time, the fight for women's suffrage—the right to vote—was in full swing. In 1886, Tarbell edited an article by Mary Lowe Dickinson that claimed women had registered only 334 patents. Tarbell was disturbed enough by the article to

TARBELL AND SUFFRAGE

Although Tarbell worked outside the home and never married or had children, she believed a woman's main role should be in the home. She did not support women's suffrage, in part because she did not think women's value depended on the ability to vote. She disagreed with suffragists who felt many of the world's evils would be remedied simply by giving women the vote. Tarbell was not the only woman of her time to feel this way. Other prominent anti-suffragists included novelist Mary Ward and children's author Kate Douglas Wiggin, as well as Annie Nathan Meyer, who helped found Barnard College for women. Many anti-suffragists, including Tarbell, still supported a woman's right to higher education.

publish a response. She felt it was wrong of suffragists to diminish the achievements of women from the past to further their cause. After careful research of patent records in Washington, DC, Tarbell reported that, in fact, women had been issued almost 2,000 patents.

Through her work at the *Chautauquan*, Tarbell discovered a love of journalism. She felt, "At last knew what I wanted to do. . . . My early absorption in rocks and plants had veered to as intense an interest in human beings."[2] She applied the same rigorous research techniques she had used in studying science to her writing.

A Writer in Paris

By 1891, Tarbell was ready for a new challenge. While writing for the *Chautauquan*, she had developed an interest in several female figures from the French Revolution (1787–1799). She decided to move to Paris, France, to continue her research into Marie-Jeanne Roland, a revolutionary who had been sent to her death on the guillotine by her political opponents.

Tarbell arrived in Paris in the summer of 1891. In addition to researching Roland, she attended lectures at the Sorbonne, Paris's famed university. There, she learned techniques for conducting historical research and fact-checking. To support herself financially, Tarbell sent articles to several American newspapers.

A New Offer

Among those who purchased some of Tarbell's articles was Samuel S. McClure. He had started a syndicate in the 1880s. He purchased articles from writers and then sold those articles to newspapers across the country. McClure was especially impressed by Tarbell's article "The Paving of the Streets of Paris by Monsieur Alphand," which described how the Parisians carried out large public works projects. After reading the article, McClure told his business partner, John Phillips, "This girl can write. I want to get her to do some work for the magazine."[3]

The magazine was a new venture he and Phillips were launching, *McClure's*

SAMUEL S. MCCLURE

Born in Ireland in 1857, Samuel S. McClure immigrated to the United States with his brothers and widowed mother in 1866. The family settled in Indiana, where his mother struggled to provide for them. When McClure was 14, he left home for the city of Valparaiso, Indiana, where he entered high school and took a position doing chores in a wealthy man's home in return for room and board. Afterward, McClure attended Knox College in Galesburg, Illinois, and became editor of the campus newspaper. Following college, he took positions with various magazines before deciding to start his own syndicate and, later, magazine. Among the *McClure's* staff, McClure was known for being excitable and full of ideas—not all of them good. But as Tarbell told the staff, "His one hundredth idea is a stroke of genius. Be on hand to grasp that one hundredth idea!"[4]

Magazine. McClure wanted to create a magazine for the average middle-class person—one that cost only fifteen cents per issue at a time when most other magazines cost thirty-five cents. He would sell advertising to make up the difference. McClure's goal for the magazine was "to deal with important social, economic, and political questions, to present the new and great inventions and discoveries, to give the best in literature" and to become "a power in the land . . . a power for good."[5]

To do this, McClure planned to hire the best writers and pay them a regular salary. Most magazines and newspapers of the time paid their writers by the word or column inch. This meant reporters could not take a lot of time researching their articles. To get paid, they had to keep churning out copy. With a regular salary, McClure's writers could spend weeks, months, or even years researching an article without going broke.

Samuel S. McClure led the charge in investigative journalism by publishing muckraking pieces.

While on a scheduled trip to Paris in 1892, McClure stopped to see Tarbell. He asked her to return to the United States to take a position on his magazine staff. Although Tarbell declined the invitation, saying she wanted to finish her research on Roland first, she did agree to send McClure articles for his new magazine.

Staff Writer

Tarbell returned to the United States in the summer of 1894. She became a staff writer at the *McClure's* office in New York City. The first issue of *McClure's* had been published in June 1893 to much acclaim. The *Review of Reviews* gave the magazine "a place among the winners."[6] The *Providence Journal* said *McClure's* was "not an imitation of anything existing in this country."[7]

With the magazine off to a successful start, McClure assigned Tarbell to write a biography of the former French emperor Napoleon Bonaparte. The first article in Tarbell's Napoleon series ran in the November 1894 issue of *McClure's*, and the series continued through June 1895. Tarbell told Napoleon's life story and gave her own assessment of his character.

Tarbell's Napoleon articles were enormously popular. During the course of the series, *McClure's Magazine*'s circulation doubled from 40,000 to 80,000 readers.[8] Because McClure was one of the few publishers of the time to give his writers a prominent byline, people began recognizing Tarbell's name.

Life of Lincoln

After the success of the Napoleon series, McClure assigned Tarbell to write a biography of Abraham Lincoln, who had been assassinated 30 years earlier. Tarbell traveled through Kentucky, Illinois, and Washington, DC, tracing the course of Lincoln's life. She reviewed court records and old newspapers. She interviewed people who had known Lincoln during his lifetime. Through her careful digging, Tarbell uncovered more than 300 previously unpublished speeches and letters by Lincoln.

Tarbell's first Lincoln article appeared in *McClure's* in November 1895. The final installment of the series ran the following November. The series pushed the magazine's circulation to more than 300,000.[9]

War

On February 15, 1898, the US battleship *Maine* exploded off the Spanish-held territory of Cuba. The cause of the explosion was never determined, but many Americans assumed the Spanish had attacked the ship. Two months later, the United States declared war on Spain.

The declaration of war changed the face of *McClure's*. McClure canceled all plans for the June 1898 issue and instead produced a special war edition. Tarbell covered the White House, while McClure deployed other reporters as war correspondents. While yellow journalists working for other publications sensationalized the war, *McClure's* provided balanced coverage and in-depth analysis. The magazine's circulation grew to 400,000.[10]

By July, the United States had defeated Spain. But the war's effects on *McClure's* were long-lasting. As Tarbell later wrote, "*McClure's* suddenly was a part of active, public life. Having tasted blood, it could no longer be content with being merely attractive, readable. It was a citizen and wanted to do a citizen's part."[11]

The Spanish-American War sent *McClure's* in a new direction.

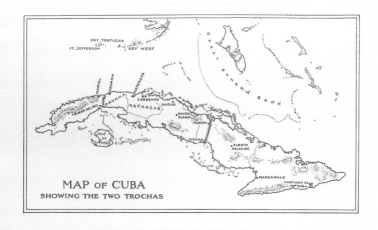

MCCLURE'S MAGAZINE.

VOL. XI.   JUNE, 1898.   NO. 2.

MAP OF CUBA
SHOWING THE TWO TROCHAS

A NEW PHOTO PROCESS

One reason magazines such as *McClure's* could offer their publications for fifteen cents per issue was the development of the new technology of photoengraving. Before this time, publications had to rely on woodcut prints to reproduce illustrations. Producing woodcuts was a time-consuming and expensive process. First, an artist had to be hired to make a drawing. Next, the drawing was engraved into a wooden block, which was then covered with ink to reproduce images on paper.

The development of the photoengraving process allowed photographs to be directly reproduced in the pages of a magazine, saving both time and money. Photoengraving worked by etching a photographic image onto a metal printing plate using acid. In 1869, halftone photoengraving was introduced. This process, which broke images into dots, allowed for the use of shades of gray.

Photoengraving has continued to develop since the time *McClure's* was popular. Today, printers still use halftones. It is one of the least expensive printing methods. Other printing options include using one color, two colors, or four colors, the last of which is most expensive. The photoengraving plates printers use to print in color are usually made of metal or plastic. In the United States, printers tend to use plates made from copper.

Workers use cameras to create photos for photoengraving reproduction.

CHAPTER FOUR

THE STANDARD OIL COMPANY

As the United States entered the 1900s, the country was very different than it had been 100 years before. The Industrial Revolution had swept the nation, bringing with it advances in technology, transportation, energy, and industry. These advances brought new prosperity to the country as it became the world's leading manufacturer.

But for 40 million Americans—more than half the US population—life was as hard as ever.[1] With factories springing up across the country, masses of people moved from country farms to crowded cities. Immigrants from around the world flooded those cities as well, looking for jobs and new opportunities. For

The Industrial Revolution opened up many jobs, including for women.

many, work was hard to come by. And even those who managed to find employment often faced dangerous, dirty conditions, working long hours for little pay. Many men did not make enough money to support their families, leading their wives and children to seek factory work as well.

Even as laborers struggled to get by, a growing middle class enjoyed the new products coming out of the Industrial Revolution, including telephones and electric lights. And business owners such as John D. Rockefeller, J. P. Morgan, Cornelius Vanderbilt, and Andrew Carnegie accumulated huge fortunes.

Exploring Trusts

In the face of the growing divide between rich and poor, the staff of *McClure's* began tackling some of the injustices they saw around them. They especially wanted to cover the topic of trusts—large corporations that owned numerous smaller, related companies. As they swallowed up their competition, these trusts became monopolies, virtually controlling entire industries, including iron, oil, railroads, and steel. With so much of an industry under their control, trusts could raise the prices of products, cut wages to workers, and manipulate shipping rates, all of which helped them maximize their profits.

Up to that point, the government had done little to regulate business, and many Americans were beginning to express concern over the growing control of trusts, even though most did not really understand exactly what trusts were. To better explain how a trust operates, the *McClure's* staff decided to present the history of a particular company. After much discussion, they settled on Standard Oil. With her childhood experiences in the oil fields, Tarbell was the obvious choice to write the story.

Relying on Records

In the years since Tarbell had first encountered Standard Oil, the company had become enormous, with operations spread across the country. In addition to refineries, the company also owned 20,000 oil wells, 4,000 miles (6,400 km) of pipelines, and 5,000 oil

WEALTH AGAINST COMMONWEALTH

Tarbell was not the first reporter to write about Standard Oil. In 1881, Henry Demarest Lloyd had published an article in the *Atlantic Monthly* that examined the practices of monopolies, with Standard Oil as an example. In 1894, Lloyd published *Wealth against Commonwealth*, which further attacked monopolies. The book received little attention. Tarbell had read it and thought it was terrific. But while Lloyd thought the answer was to turn to socialism, Tarbell had other ideas. "As I saw it, it was not capitalism but an open disregard of decent ethical business practices by capitalists which lay at the bottom of the story," she wrote.[2]

tank railcars.[3] Standard Oil controlled almost 90 percent of the oil industry in the United States.[4]

With its huge presence, Standard Oil had faced plenty of legal challenges. Courts in several states had challenged Standard Oil's monopoly. Records from these hearings became invaluable to Tarbell as she began her research in the fall of 1901. She traveled to Washington, DC, New York, Pennsylvania, Ohio, and Kansas tracking them down. She also reviewed pages of testimony given before congressional committees, as well as newspaper articles and pamphlets.

Interview with a Magnate

In addition to reading hundreds of thousands of pages, Tarbell conducted interviews with government officials and the company's competitors. Once she had enough information, she also confronted Standard Oil insiders. When people asked her why she had not gone to Standard officials first, Tarbell said,

> The Standard Oil Company would have shut the door of their closet on their skeleton. But after one had discovered the skeleton and had scrutinized him at very close range, why then shut the door?[5]

The company officers she initially talked to gave vague answers and little information. Then, a Standard Oil vice president, Henry Rogers, offered to meet with Tarbell. She agreed. And she was nervous. Tarbell had interviewed plenty of powerful people in her day. But, as she said,

> This was my first high-ranking captain of industry. Was I putting my head into a lion's mouth? . . . It was one thing to tackle the Standard Oil Company in documents, as I had been doing, quite another thing to meet it face to face.[6]

But when she arrived at Rogers's house, Tarbell was immediately put at ease by the stately looking 62-year-old man. As the two began to talk, they discovered an immediate connection: Rogers had owned a small refinery in Rouseville while Tarbell was growing up there.

As she talked with Rogers, Tarbell found him generally open to answering her questions. Over the next two years, Tarbell and Rogers continued to meet, usually at the Standard Oil offices on Broadway in New York

SPYING IN CHURCH

As she wrote her Standard Oil pieces, Tarbell thought she needed a better feel for the man who ran the company. But she never got an interview with Rockefeller, and he rarely went out in public. So, in 1903, she, an assistant, and a sketch artist snuck into a Sunday service at Rockefeller's church. Tarbell used her observations as the basis of a 1905 profile of Rockefeller. In it, she called him a "living mummy" whose image showed "concentration, craftiness, cruelty, and something indefinably repulsive."[7]

Henry Rogers proved a good resource for Tarbell's series about Standard Oil.

City. At their meetings, Tarbell would present evidence she had accumulated, and Rogers would be given the opportunity to explain the company's decisions. But Tarbell made sure Rogers was clear on one point—in the end, her judgments would appear in the articles, not his.

Tarbell's Series about Standard Oil

Even as she continued her interviews with Rogers, Tarbell sorted through her piles of research to begin writing her articles. She had drafts of the first three ready by May

1902. She gave the drafts to McClure and Phillips, who edited them relentlessly. McClure read each of Tarbell's manuscripts three times. If he became bored by the third reading, he asked her to rewrite it. Tarbell willingly returned to the manuscript again and again, revising the material until it was ready for publication.

The first article in Tarbell's Standard Oil series was published in the November 1902 issue of *McClure's*. "The Birth of an Industry" traces the beginning of the oil industry in Pennsylvania and chronicles the lives of the young men who had come to the region to set up small wells and refineries. She concludes the article with a cliffhanger: "Life ran swift and ruddy and joyous in these men. . . . Suddenly, . . . a big hand reached out . . . to steal their conquest and throttle their future."[8]

That hand, of course, belonged to Rockefeller and his Standard Oil Company, and in the ensuing articles, Tarbell examines how Rockefeller had taken over the oil industry. She reveals the company's use of illegal railroad rebates, bribery, and intimidation to drive independent oilmen out of business. Tarbell recounts the story of the Oil War of 1872 and tells how many refiners had no choice but to sell to Rockefeller for less than half of what their businesses were worth. Those who refused were threatened with financial ruin.

In the February 1904 installment, "Cutting to Kill," Tarbell accuses Standard Oil of using corporate espionage to hurt its competitors. She gives evidence company officials paid off railroad clerks to inform them of competitors' shipments. Standard officials then undercut their competitors' prices and even went so far as to threaten vendors into canceling orders from competing oil companies. In this article, as in the others in the series, Tarbell prints many of the documents she used to make her case, allowing readers to analyze the evidence for themselves. After the publication of "Cutting to Kill," an

An artist drew those getting rich from the oil industry as pirates.

angered Rogers refused to hold further interviews with Tarbell.

Despite all of Standard Oil's faults, Tarbell also points out the company's "legitimate greatness."[9] As she acknowledges,

> "It was not long before I was saying to myself, . . . You are a part of this democratic system they are trying to make work. Is it not your business to use your profession to serve it?"[12]
>
> —Ida Tarbell, All in the Day's Work, 1939

> Something besides illegal advantages had gone into the making of the Standard Oil Trust. . . . This huge bulk, blackened by commercial sin, was strong in all great business qualities—in energy, in intelligence, in dauntlessness.[10]

In her concluding article, published in October 1904, Tarbell issues a challenge to her readers:

> And what are we going to do about it? For it is our business. We the people of the United States and nobody else must cure whatever is wrong in the industrial situation, typified by this narrative of the growth of the Standard Oil Company.[11]

Reaction

Tarbell hoped her articles would arouse Rockefeller to make some sort of response. But he followed Standard Oil's policy of remaining silent in the face of criticism. In private, however, Rockefeller called Tarbell a "misguided woman" and "Miss Tar Barrel."[13] Standard Oil also sponsored the distribution of pamphlets praising the virtues of the company and criticizing Tarbell. One called her "honest, bitter, talented, prejudiced, and disappointed."[14] A few newspapers loyal to Rockefeller also tore apart Tarbell's articles. The *Oil City Derrick* described her as a "hysterical woman."[15]

But most critics were full of praise for Tarbell's work. The *Washington Times* said she had "proven herself to be one of the most commanding figures in American letters."[16] In November 1904, Tarbell's series was published as a two-volume book called *The History of the Standard Oil Company*. It quickly became a best seller. And Tarbell became, according to McClure, "The most famous woman in America."[17]

LEFT OUT

Despite the success of her Standard Oil series, which had made her one of the best-known journalists of the day, Tarbell was left out of the first annual publishers' dinner. Held for magazine publishers, editors, and writers, the dinner featured President Theodore Roosevelt as the keynote speaker. But the guest list included only men. As Tarbell told her colleague Ray Stannard Baker, "It is the first time since I came into the office that the fact of petticoats has stood in my way, and I am half inclined to resent it."[18]

THE HISTORY OF
THE STANDARD OIL COMPANY

BY

IDA M. TARBELL

AUTHOR OF

THE LIFE OF ABRAHAM LINCOLN, THE LIFE OF NAPOLEON BONAPARTE,
AND MADAME ROLAND: A BIOGRAPHICAL STUDY

ILLUSTRATED WITH PORTRAITS
PICTURES AND DIAGRAMS

Ida Tarbell's series about Standard Oil is part of the foundation of
investigative journalism.

CHAPTER FIVE

DAWN OF THE MUCKRAKERS

With her Standard Oil series, Tarbell established a new kind of journalism. Today, this type of journalism is more commonly known as investigative journalism. At the time, it became known as muckraking because the writers sought out and sorted through the details of muck, which consisted of scandalous or bad stories.

Historians generally consider the muckraking era to have begun with the publication of the January 1903 issue of *McClure's*. The third of Tarbell's Standard Oil articles appeared in that issue, along with investigative articles by two other *McClure's* writers, Ray Stannard Baker and Lincoln

Tarbell's experience, thoroughness, and writing skills made her a force in the news business.

LINCOLN STEFFENS

Born on April 6, 1866, to a wealthy family, Lincoln Steffens grew up in a mansion in San Francisco, California. The pampered Steffens was a poor student, largely because he did not enjoy the structured environment of a classroom. But during a college history class, he was assigned a research project using original documents. He found the work fascinating, and after traveling to Europe for graduate studies, he returned to the United States to work as a reporter for the *New York Evening Post*. He followed that with a position at the *Commercial Advertiser* before joining the staff of *McClure's* in 1901. Tarbell admired Steffens, describing him as "coolly determined to demonstrate to men and women of good will and honest purpose what they were up against."[3]

Steffens. In an editorial for the issue, McClure points out that all three of these articles highlight the "American contempt of law."[1] He further implores people to take action to fix the problems the articles address: "There is no one left: none but all of us. . . . We forget that we all are the people."[2]

Steffens's article for the January 1903 issue was "The Shame of Minneapolis." It was part of Shame of the Cities, a series about political corruption. Steffens had begun researching the series shortly after joining the staff of *McClure's* in 1901. The first article, "Tweed Days in St. Louis," ran in the October 1902 issue. In it, Steffens points out how political bosses—men who did not hold elected positions but used bribery and other illegal methods to manipulate votes—ran the city of Saint Louis. In "The Shame of Minneapolis," the second article in the series, Steffens describes how the mayor of that city had fired half the police force in order to sell their positions to those willing to pay for them. Then the mayor allowed illegal businesses such as saloons and gambling rings to operate in the city for a fee.

Meanwhile, Baker's article for the January 1903 *McClure's* examines a coal miners' strike in eastern Pennsylvania. For the article, "The Right to Work," Baker talked with some of the thousands of men who continued to work despite the strike. These men faced physical attacks, vandalism of their homes, and death threats from striking workers.

More Muckraking

With the success of the January 1903 issue of *McClure's*—it sold out

> "The journalist is a true servant of democracy. The best journalist of today occupies the exact place of the prophets of old: he cries out the truth and calls for reform."[6]
>
> —Ray Stannard Baker, 1906

within days—other magazines quickly adopted the investigative style of journalism. Along with *McClure's*, *Cosmopolitan* and *Munsey's* became the most prominent muckraking magazines. Other monthly publications also began including investigative pieces, including *Collier's*, *Everybody's*, *Leslie's*, *Pearson's*, and *Hampton's*.

Taking a cue from *McClure's*, many of these magazines began to pay their writers regular salaries so they could devote the time needed to carry out thorough research. From 1903 to 1912, these magazines published nearly 2,000 investigative articles.[5] Most of them were written by a small group of writers that included Tarbell, Steffens, and Baker, along with Upton Sinclair, David Graham Phillips, and a handful of others.

Upton Sinclair and *The Jungle*

Not all muckraking pieces were nonfiction. In 1904, the weekly socialist publication *Appeal to Reason* hired freelance writer Upton Sinclair to write about working conditions in the slaughterhouses of Chicago, Illinois. Sinclair wanted to present a firsthand account of

Tarbell, *front left*, and her colleagues paved the way for other writers seeking to expose injustices.

Packingtown, as Chicago's meatpacking district was known, so he donned worn-out clothes and carried a lunch pail. Looking like this, he was able to slip into and out of slaughterhouses, observing and talking to the workers in them. He even lived in the rundown workers' tenements, where he got to know the everyday problems slaughterhouse workers and their families faced. For seven weeks, Sinclair "went about white-faced and thin, partly from undernourishment, partly from horror," he later wrote.[7]

With his research complete, Sinclair presented what he had found in the form of a novel, which was serialized in *Appeal to Reason* in 1905 and published as a book called *The Jungle* in 1906. The novel follows the story of Lithuanian immigrant Jurgis Rudkus and his family as they lived and worked in Packingtown. The characters faced horrible conditions in the slaughterhouses. Rudkus worked in a room at 100 degrees Fahrenheit (38°C) where extra animal parts were ground to make fertilizer:

> The phosphates soaked in through every pore of Jurgis' skin, and in five minutes, he had a headache, and in fifteen was almost dazed. The blood was pounding in his brain like an engine's throbbing; there was a frightful pain in the top of his skull, and he could hardly control his hands. . . . At the end of that day of horror, he could scarcely stand.[8]

In addition to drawing attention to the terrible working conditions in the slaughterhouses, Sinclair also describes the unsanitary conditions on the slaughterhouse floor, where rats ran freely over piles of meat. "These rats were nuisances, and the packers would put poisoned bread out for them; they would die, and then rats, bread, and meat would go into the hoppers together" to make sausage.[9] The novel concludes with Rudkus joining the Socialist Party, reflecting Sinclair's own belief that socialism was the answer to the problems of US society.

David Graham Phillips and the Senate

In February 1906, *Cosmopolitan* magazine published the first in a nine-part series called the Treason of the Senate

PUBLICATIONS: 1890–1920

The number of newspapers and magazines published in the United States grew rapidly during the muckraking era, with hundreds of new publications popping up each year. The number of publications began declining after World War I (1914–1918).

YEAR	NUMBER OF NEWSPAPERS AND PERIODICALS[10]
1890	17,712
1892	19,214
1894	19,855
1896	20,255
1898	21,061
1900	21,325
1902	21,708
1904	22,223
1906	22,392
1908	22,455
1910	22,725
1912	22,837
1914	22,977
1916	23,024
1918	22,842
1920	21,012

by David Graham Phillips. At that time, members of the US Senate were appointed by state legislatures rather than elected by citizens. Phillips charges that these legislatures were often influenced by powerful business interests. He also questions the practice of allowing senators to sit on the boards of directors of corporations and then turn around and vote on laws that might affect those corporations. Phillips names names, accusing 21 senators of having inappropriate business connections.[11] He says these senators were guilty of treason. He writes,

> *Treason is a strong word, but not too strong, rather too weak, to characterize the situation in which the Senate is the eager, resourceful, indefatigable agent of interests as hostile to the American people as any invading army could be, and vastly more dangerous.[12]*

Other Muckrakers

Among the other topics tackled by muckrakers for various magazines was the patent medicine industry. In 1904, *Ladies' Home Journal* editor Edward Bok wrote a series of articles called the "Patent-Medicine" Curse. The next year, the article "The Great American Fraud" by Samuel Hopkins Adams appeared in *Collier's* magazine.

These articles explore the $100-million-a-year industry and expose the fact that many patent medicines

Collier's

THE NATIONAL WEEKLY

Patent medicine was a popular topic for
journalists in the early 1900s.

included dangerous quantities of alcohol, morphine, cocaine, and other drugs.[13] As Bok points out,

A mother who would hold up her hands in holy horror at the thought of her child drinking a glass of beer, which contains from two to five percent of alcohol, gives to that child with her own hands a patent medicine that contains from seventeen to forty-four percent of alcohol—to say nothing of opium and cocaine![14]

Child labor was another frequently covered topic. In 1906, Edwin Markham wrote a series about this topic for *Cosmopolitan.* He discusses the conditions faced by millions of children who worked 10 to 14 hours a day (or night) for a dime. Soon after Markham's work was printed, John Spargo published *The Bitter Cry of the Children.* In this book, he describes child labor in coal mines, where boys as young as 10 or 12 sat hunched over all day, picking pieces of slate out of coal rushing by in chutes. Spargo writes,

THREE TEASPOONS

Throughout the 1700s and 1800s, patent medicines flourished across America. They were sold over the counter to cure a variety of illnesses. Even oil was bottled and sold under names including "American Medicinal Oil." Oil-based patent medicines were said to cure cholera morbus, a stomach illness causing cramps, diarrhea, and vomiting. Oil was also supposed to help with liver and lung problems. Patients were told to take three teaspoons of the oil three times a day.

Accidents to the hands, such as cut, broken, or crushed
fingers, are common among the boys. Sometimes there is
a worse accident: a terrified shriek is heard, and a boy is
mangled and torn in the machinery, or disappears in the
chute to be picked out later smothered and dead.[15]

Over time, muckrakers exposed corporate and political corruption, poverty, dangerous working conditions, fraud, race relations, women's issues, environmental problems, organized crime, and more. Even as they wrote about the ills of society, most of these writers maintained a factual tone, keeping their own outrage below the surface of their words.

> "I could do one thing. I could write. I could try to make other people see what I had seen, feel what I had felt. I wanted to make others as angry as I was."[16]
>
> —Mary Heaton Vorse, journalist, 1912

CHAPTER SIX

THE PROGRESSIVE ERA

Part of the reason the muckrakers were so successful was the timing of their appearance. Up until the late 1800s, the US government had practiced the concept of laissez-faire, a word taken from French that means "allow to do." A laissez-faire government interferes as little as possible in business, the economy, and social concerns. But in approximately 1900, many Americans began calling for the government to address some of the problems that had crept into society. These calls for reforms led later historians to term the early 1900s the Progressive Era.

Investigative journalists helped push the US government, led by President Theodore Roosevelt, to make changes to help Americans.

The Progressive Era was, as Theodore Roosevelt said, a time of "fierce discontent."[1] Progressives believed government involvement was necessary to remedy inequality. They wanted the government to improve living standards for the millions of working poor while also restricting the almost unlimited power of big businesses.

Many of those who supported the Progressive movement were members of the middle class—the same people who made up the majority of the audience of the muckraking magazines. And the topics they were concerned about were the same topics covered in the muckraking articles: child labor, political corruption, poor working conditions, poverty, and the power of big business. McClure and other magazine publishers saw the potential for their publications to inspire

THEODORE ROOSEVELT

Born on October 27, 1858, Theodore Roosevelt entered politics at age 23, when he became a Republican legislator for the state of New York. He later served as a member of the US Civil Service Commission, as police commissioner of New York City, as assistant secretary of the US Navy, and as governor of New York.

Roosevelt had little interest in becoming vice president of the United States because he believed the position held little real power, but he accepted the nomination under William McKinley. The decision led to his becoming president. With McKinley's assassination in 1901, Roosevelt automatically became president, the youngest in history. He was 42 years old.

social change. McClure said it was "up to magazines to rouse public opinion."[2]

At the same time, printing muckraking articles was profitable, because these articles were exactly what people of the time wanted to read. As reporter Walter Lippmann explained in 1914,

But the mere fact that muckraking was what people wanted to hear is in many ways the most important revelation of the whole campaign. There is no other way of explaining the quick approval which the muckrakers won. . . . They demanded a hearing; it was granted. They asked for belief; they were believed. They cried that something should be done, and there was every appearance of action.[3]

SOCIAL DARWINISM

Before the Progressive Era, many Americans believed in the theory of social Darwinism. According to this theory, Charles Darwin's theory of survival of the fittest—the best and strongest organisms survive in nature—applies to economics. Social Darwinists believe those who achieve financial success are smarter or more driven than the poor. They blame the poor for their own plight. Progressives rejected this argument, holding instead that greed and unethical practices form the basis of success for the wealthy.

By 1905, more than 5 million Americans subscribed to one muckraking magazine or another.[4]

A Reform President

The Progressive cause received a huge boost when
Theodore Roosevelt became president in 1901. Roosevelt
had been vice president under William McKinley, who
was shot on September 6, 1901, and died eight days later.
The reform-minded Roosevelt delivered his first annual
message to Congress on December 3, 1901. In it, he spoke
of the need for reform:

> *The captains of industry who have driven the railway
> systems across this continent, who have built up our
> commerce, who have developed our manufactures, have
> on the whole done great good to our people. . . . Yet it is
> also true that there are real and grave evils [in American
> business] . . . and a resolute and practical effort must be
> made to correct these evils.*[5]

Throughout his presidency, Roosevelt openly
interacted with the press. In fact, he coined the term *bully
pulpit* to refer to the ability of the president to shape public
thought through the media. To maintain good relations
with reporters, Roosevelt set up a special room for them
in the West Wing of the White House. He allowed them
to ask questions during his midday shave or as he signed
documents at the end of the day. Roosevelt was especially
close to several muckrakers, including Tarbell, Baker, and

Steffens. He once wrote to Baker and complimented the journalist's work:

> *I have learned to look to your articles for real help. You have impressed me with your earnest desire to be fair, with your freedom from hysteria, and with your anxiety to tell the truth rather than to write something that will be sensational.*[6]

In addition to admiring the muckraking journalists, Roosevelt was assisted by them. Their articles helped raise public awareness of the social issues. The resulting calls for reform helped Roosevelt push his policies through Congress.

"I have only one principle, and that is represented by an effort to make it harder for the rich to grow richer and easier for the poor to keep from growing poorer."[7]

—E. W. Scripps, newspaper publisher, 1910

Breaking Up the Trusts

Even before the muckrakers began writing their exposés, Congress had passed the Sherman Antitrust Act in 1890. This act was meant to regulate trusts and prevent monopolies, but Congress allocated little money to enforce the law. And loopholes allowed trusts to get around it.

With muckrakers stirring up public outcry against the trusts, however, Roosevelt pushed for stronger

One artist depicted the muckrakers as crusaders fighting for social justices, their pens serving as swords.

regulation. In 1903, after Tarbell's Standard Oil articles had begun appearing, Congress passed several antitrust measures, including the establishment of the Department of Commerce and Labor, which had the authority to investigate any corporation involved in interstate commerce. Other antitrust measures passed that year included a bill outlawing railroad rebates and one giving precedence on court schedules to suits against companies accused of violating the Sherman Antitrust Act. Roosevelt openly acknowledged his success in finally passing these antitrust measures was because "a great many people had been thinking and talking" about trusts, thanks to Tarbell's articles.[8]

The Suit against Standard Oil

With antitrust laws strengthened, Roosevelt's administration went after the Standard Oil Trust. On November 15, 1906, the US attorney general, the government's lawyer, filed an antitrust suit against Standard Oil. Using evidence from Tarbell's articles to conduct its own investigation, the government accused Standard Oil of a variety of illegal practices, including holding a monopoly, participating in an illegal railroad rebate scheme, manipulating prices, and spying on competitors.

In 1909, a federal circuit court ruled against Standard Oil. The company appealed its case to the US Supreme Court, but on May 15, 1911, the Supreme Court upheld the original court's decision. Standard Oil was ordered to sell the

RACIAL INEQUALITY

In 1908, Baker wrote a series that was later published as the book *Following the Color Line*. Baker's book documented the plight of blacks in the South, who faced legal segregation. Baker also demonstrated how discrimination had crept as far north as Boston, Massachusetts. "Several hotels, restaurants, and especially confectionary stores, will not serve Negroes," he wrote. "The discrimination is not made openly, but a Negro who goes to such places is informed that there are no accommodations, or he is overlooked and otherwise slighted, so that he does not come again."[9] Baker was one of the few muckrakers of his era to address such racial inequalities.

33 subsidiary companies it owned. This brought Standard Oil's monopoly of the oil industry to an end. It also made Rockefeller the first billionaire in the United States when he profited from the selling of the subsidiaries.

Other Reforms

Muckraking articles helped inspire other reforms as well. Stories about the unhealthy living conditions of the urban poor brought about the creation of New York's Tenement House Commission in 1900. The next year, the state's Tenement House Law established minimum requirements for the size and ventilation of tenement rooms. At the national level, articles about child labor inspired the establishment of the National Child Labor Committee in 1907 and eventually led to federal laws banning child labor.

While Sinclair had hoped *The Jungle* would also inspire reforms to benefit poor workers, he found the novel instead led to an outcry against unsanitary conditions in slaughterhouses. "I aimed at the public's heart, and by accident I hit it in the stomach," Sinclair said.[10] The uproar resulting from the publication of *The Jungle*, along with growing concerns over patent medicines, led to passage of the Pure Food and Drug Act of 1906.

Upton Sinclair, photographed in 1962 when he was 90 years old, spent his career fighting for social justice and won a Pulitzer Prize for one of his many books, the novel *Dragon's Teeth*.

Attacking Political Corruption

In addition to leading to the establishment of new laws, muckraking articles also helped change the face of politics. Steffens's articles about corrupt local officials led many of those officials to be removed from office.

In addition, Phillips's articles about corruption in the US Senate added to already growing pressures to change the way US senators were elected. In 1913, the Seventeenth Amendment to the US Constitution ensured the election of senators by popular vote.

CHAPTER SEVEN

END OF THE MUCKRAKERS

Despite all the reforms the muckrakers helped him achieve, President Roosevelt was sometimes concerned about the negative tone of muckraking articles, as well as their repeated focus on corrupt businesses. In 1905, Roosevelt sent McClure a letter, writing,

> It is an unfortunate thing to encourage people to believe that all crimes are connected with business. . . . I wish very much that you could have articles showing up the hideous iniquity of which mobs are guilty, the wrongs of violence by the poor as well as the wrongs of corruption by the rich.[1]

Although *McClure's* complied to some extent, other publications did not. The next

David Graham Phillips's articles angered Roosevelt and also inspired passage of the Seventeenth Amendment.

year, Roosevelt was particularly angered by Phillips's
Treason of the Senate series in *Cosmopolitan*. Phillips
named some of the president's political allies among the
corrupt senators. On March 17, 1906, Roosevelt delivered
a speech at a meeting of the Gridiron Club—a gathering
of reporters, politicians, and business leaders. He
condemned journalists who focused on sensational stories
while "ignoring at the same time the good in the world."[2]

Although the speech was supposed to be off the
record, word of what Roosevelt said quickly spread.
Steffens thought the president had hurt himself as much
as the reform journalists with his comments. He told
the president, "Well, you have put an end to all these
journalistic investigations that have made you."[3]

Baker was also upset by the president's remarks. When
he learned Roosevelt planned to repeat his speech publicly,
Baker wrote the president a letter to warn him that "such
an attack might greatly injure the work which we were
trying honestly to do."[4] Roosevelt insisted his attack was
not against the *McClure's* writers but those journalists who
printed carelessly researched, sensational articles. But
Baker said the honest journalists would be the first to stop
writing in the face of such attacks, leaving behind the
"outright ranters and inciters."[5]

Despite Steffens's and Baker's concerns, Roosevelt publicly repeated the speech on April 14. The president compared investigative journalists to a character in John Bunyan's popular novel *The Pilgrim's Progress*. In the story, the character of the Man with the Muck-rake never looks up from raking the floor and "consistently refuses to see aught [anything] that is lofty," according to Roosevelt.[6] The president went on to say,

> There is filth on the floor, and it must be scraped up with the muck-rake. . . . But the man who never does anything else, who never thinks or speaks or writes, save of his feats with the muck-rake, speedily becomes, not a help to society, . . . but one of the most potent forces for evil.[7]

With his speech, Roosevelt coined the term *muckraker* to describe journalists who printed investigative pieces. Some journalists accepted the term with pride. Others, including Tarbell, were hurt. She later said, "To my

MISUSE OF *MUCKRAKER*

In her 1939 autobiography, Tarbell pointed out that Roosevelt had misread *The Pilgrim's Progress*. The Man with the Muck-rake had his eyes focused on the ground because it was covered with treasure, not filth. He refused to look up for fear of losing his riches. Thus, she said, "The president would have been nearer Bunyan's meaning if he had named the rich sinners of the times . . . 'muckrakers of great wealth.'"[8] Despite Roosevelt's error, the term stuck.

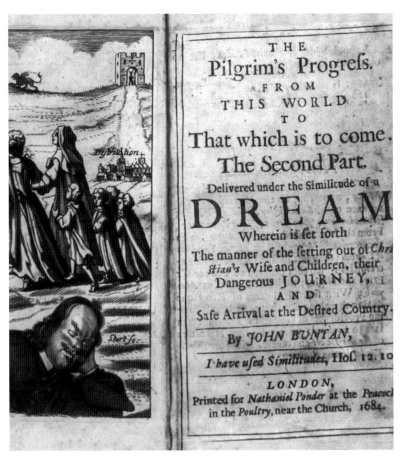

Roosevelt got the word *muckraker* from the book *The Pilgrim's Progress,*
which was published in England in 1684.

chagrin, I found myself included in a new school, that of
the muckrakers."[9]

Baker was also disheartened. He later wrote of his
reaction: "It was difficult for me to understand this attack,
considering all that had recently happened, all that the
President owed to investigations and reports of at least
some of the magazine writers."[10]

Changes in the Magazine World

Only a month after the president's speech, life at *McClure's* changed forever. On May 11, Tarbell, Steffens, Baker, John Phillips, and an editor named Albert Boyden announced they were leaving *McClure's* to form their own magazine. Although many assumed the announcement had something to do with Roosevelt's speech, the move had been coming for months. Tarbell and the other staff members had become unhappy with McClure's increasingly erratic leadership and his plans to expand the magazine into other business ventures.

The group purchased *American Magazine*. As the Kansas City, Missouri, *Independent* noted, the world would now see what happened with "all the muckrakers muckraking under one tent."[11] But while Tarbell and the others planned to write muckraking pieces for their new magazine, they also pledged to make "this new

THE FATE OF *MCCLURE'S*

Although Tarbell and the other *McClure's* staffers almost immediately set up a competing magazine upon leaving, there were no hard feelings between them and McClure. McClure gave the departing writers several months' salary—and he felt that was not enough. Losing his staff, McClure said, was "the greatest tragedy thus far of my life," but he soon hired new reporters.[12] In 1911, McClure sold the company. He retired soon afterward. He and the original *McClure's* staff remained friends the rest of their lives.

American Magazine . . . the most stirring and delightful monthly book of fiction, humor, sentiment, and joyous reading that is anywhere published. It will reflect a happy, struggling, fighting world, in which, as we believe, good people are coming out on top."[13]

The first issue of *American Magazine* hit newsstands in October 1906. Over the next few years, the magazine covered taxes, race relations, politics, and the 12-hour workday in the steel industry. On a more positive note, the magazine published accounts of successful reforms, as well as stories about honest politicians and businesses that could serve as examples to others.

Although *American Magazine* met with success, Tarbell realized it was not the same as working at *McClure's*. In 1911, she and the other owners sold their financial interest in the magazine. In 1915, Tarbell and the former *McClure's* reporters resigned.

LIFE AFTER MUCKRAKING

After leaving *American Magazine*, Tarbell continued writing freelance pieces for several publications. She traveled the country delivering lectures about war, politics, and trusts. In 1939, she published her autobiography, *All in the Day's Work*. Tarbell died on January 6, 1944, at the age of 86.

A Quiet End

By the time the muckrakers left *American Magazine*, the muckraking era had been in decline for almost a decade. Roosevelt's 1906 speech had begun a period of decreased circulation for most muckraking magazines as the public seemed to tire of reading about problems.

The muckraking magazines themselves also became a factor in the decline of muckraking. Many had grown into large businesses that relied heavily on advertising revenue. As a result, some editors were careful not to print articles critical of their advertisers.

The country's spirit of reform shifted as well with the end of Roosevelt's presidency in 1909. William Howard Taft, who took office after Roosevelt, continued some of Roosevelt's reform agenda but met with limited success. This was in part because of his inability to engage the press and the public as Roosevelt had. In 1914, the public's attention turned to World War I (1914–1918), which had broken out in Europe and would soon involve the United States. Newspapers and magazines devoted their pages to covering the war.

The muckraking era, which many considered a golden age of journalism, had come to an end. But investigative journalism was only beginning.

"It was not long before I was saying to myself, . . . You are a part of this democratic system they are trying to make work. Is it not your business to use your profession to serve it?"[14]

—*Ida Tarbell,* All in the Day's Work, 1939

CHAPTER EIGHT

RESURGENCE

Although muckraking faded from US
newspapers and magazines during
World War I, Tarbell's successors in
investigative journalism have gone through
several periods of renewed vigor. In the 1930s,
a young writer for the *San Francisco News*,
John Steinbeck, reported on farmers who had
traveled from the Great Plains to California
in search of work. Severe drought and erosion
from agriculture sent dust storms raging
across the Great Plains, an event known as
the Dust Bowl. Conditions halted farming in
many areas, causing mass migration. When the
migrants found no work, they set up camps
filled with makeshift shanties.

Steinbeck described conditions in the
camps, where cardboard houses fell apart

Conditions during the Dust Bowl made
farming nearly impossible in large areas of
the Great Plains.

in the rain to become "a brown, pulpy mush." Other houses were built "by driving willow branches into the ground and wattling [weaving] weeds, tin, old paper, and strips of carpet against them."[1] In 1939, Steinbeck channeled his experiences in the camps into the novel *The Grapes of Wrath*. Hailed as a literary masterpiece, the novel received a Pulitzer Prize and helped bring about changes in conditions for migrant farmers.

Anti-Smoking Articles

During World War II (1939–1945), newspapers focused on war coverage. But investigations made a resurgence in the 1950s. By this time, approximately 50 percent of men and 25 percent of women in the

United States smoked.[3] Although some people suspected smoking could be bad for one's health, few media outlets were willing to condemn smoking because cigarette companies provided a large source of advertising revenue.

Reader's Digest, however, did not accept advertisements, which meant it could freely criticize tobacco companies. In 1952, the magazine printed "Cancer by the Carton" by Roy Norr. In the article, Norr disclosed that lung cancer deaths in the United States had increased 144 percent from 1938 to 1948.[4] Norr further charged that the tobacco companies had known about the health dangers of smoking and had covered them up by claiming cigarettes caused only minor side effects.

The battle against tobacco companies continued for more than 50 years. Eventually, the fight ended in the courtroom, where tobacco companies were ordered to pay billions of dollars in settlements. By 2014, smoking rates had fallen to approximately 17 percent of all adults.[5]

News on TV

The advent of television news in the 1950s allowed for more immediate coverage of events. News shows such as Edward R. Murrow's See It Now became popular. In March 1954, Murrow featured a series about Senator Joseph McCarthy. The senator had been conducting a communist witch hunt among government officials, celebrities, and others. McCarthy accused many of being sympathizers of the Soviet Union. These were serious accusations because the United States and the Soviet Union were then engaged in the Cold War, a period of hostile relations that lasted from 1945 to 1991. Those accused of having communist ties were interrogated before a congressional committee and often lost their jobs and their reputations, whether or not the charges were true.

Using recordings of McCarthy's interrogations, Murrow highlighted the senator's techniques of intimidation and fear. After the show aired, Murrow received thousands of phone calls and letters of gratitude. Many called the program "television's finest hour."[6]

Edward R. Murrow brought investigative journalism to television.

Afterward, McCarthy's search came to an end, and in December 1954, the US Senate officially censured him for conduct unbecoming a senator.

Covering Up a Massacre

Around the same time as Murrow's report aired, the United States was becoming involved in the Vietnam War (1954–1975). By the late 1960s, more than 500,000 US soldiers were stationed in Vietnam, fighting a war that was unpopular at home.[7] On March 17, 1968, newspapers in the United States reported that US troops had successfully taken a Vietnamese stronghold. Only two US soldiers had been killed, compared with 128 Vietnamese.[8] And US troops had recovered only three enemy weapons.[9] This news seemed odd to veteran reporter Seymour Hersh, who suspected most of the enemy dead had been civilians.

A year and a half later, Hersh found proof. Acting on a tip, he discovered a US Army officer, William Calley, was being secretly court-martialed. Hersh interviewed Calley and learned US troops had killed 500 women, children, and elderly men in the Vietnamese village of My Lai.[11]

Hersh's story about the incident—which included tales of US soldiers burning huts with families inside—seemed too horrific for many newspapers to believe. At first, they refused to print it. The independent news agency Dispatch News Service finally agreed to distribute the story, which then appeared on the front pages of several papers. Afterward, protests against the war increased.

Watergate

Perhaps the biggest scandal ever uncovered by investigative journalists was Watergate. On June 17, 1972, police arrested five men for attempting to break into and bug the Democratic National Committee headquarters in the Watergate building complex in Washington, DC.[12] *Washington Post* reporters Bob Woodward and Carl Bernstein discovered the burglars had connections to the Republican Party and began to suspect there was more to the story than a simple break-in.

Over the next two years, the reporters investigated the Watergate scandal, ultimately printing a series of 225 articles. Their investigations revealed President Richard Nixon and members of his administration had known about the break-in and had tried to cover it up. Woodward and Bernstein also discovered evidence of other illegal activity, including money laundering and an attempt to sabotage Nixon's opponents in the upcoming election. As the evidence against him mounted, Nixon resigned the presidency in 1974. Twenty-five members of his administration were sent to prison. Meanwhile, the *Washington Post* was awarded the 1973 Pulitzer Prize for Public Service.

"Investigative reporting, no matter how excellent, cannot accomplish much all by itself. The people must respond to revealed scandal with popular revulsion and anger. It is this outrage which powers the whole process."[13]

—J. Edward Murray, former editor of the Arizona Republic, 1977

CHAPTER NINE

LEGACY OF TRUTH

The muckrakers' long tradition of investigative reporting continues today. In recent years, investigative journalists have published articles about modern meatpacking, prisoner abuse, and the treatment of wounded veterans, among other topics.

In 2001, journalist Eric Schlosser reported on the modern meatpacking industry in the book *Fast Food Nation*. He describes working conditions in modern slaughterhouses that were not all that different from those Sinclair wrote about in *The Jungle* nearly a century earlier. Schlosser found slaughterhouse employees worked long hours for little pay and often suffered injuries that were not reported.

Eric Schlosser is one of countless writers who continue the muckraking tradition.

He also contended the fast food industry was responsible for an obesity epidemic, as well as for creating a larger gap between rich and poor.

The year 2001 also marked the September 11 terrorist attacks, which led to the US wars in Afghanistan and Iraq. In 2004, *60 Minutes II* and Hersh, writing for the *New Yorker*, exposed the abuse of Iraqi prisoners by US soldiers at Abu Ghraib prison in Baghdad, Iraq. US Army officials had been aware of this abuse since 2003, when they found photographs of US soldiers torturing and humiliating prisoners. Hersh's article releases details of a secret US Army investigation into the abuse. The investigation reports soldiers "breaking chemical lights and pouring the phosphoric liquid on detainees; pouring cold water on naked detainees; beating detainees with a broom handle and a chair," and more.[1] Hersh presents further evidence that suggested the soldiers had been ordered to treat the prisoners this way in order to make them easier to interrogate. After the story broke, 11 US soldiers were convicted in military trials. Official investigations into the incident found no evidence that high-level officials were involved in the abuse, although some questioned these conclusions.

The wars in Afghanistan and Iraq also resulted in numerous injuries to US soldiers. Many of them were sent to recover at the Walter Reed Army Medical Center in Washington, DC. In 2007, *Washington Post* reporters Dana Priest and Anne Hull spent four months secretly visiting the medical facility. They published their findings in the series the Other Walter Reed. In the series, they explain how military personnel undergoing outpatient treatment were forced to recover in makeshift facilities at rundown hotels and apartments. In one article, the reporters describe the room of an injured army specialist: "Part of the wall is torn and hangs in the air, weighted down with black mold. . . . Signs of neglect are everywhere: mouse droppings, belly-up cockroaches, stained carpets, cheap mattresses."[2] The articles led to a government investigation and immediate leadership changes at the hospital.

Journalists around the World

Investigative journalism has also spread around the globe, with reporters in places such as Indonesia, China, and Angola pointing out injustices. In Indonesia, for example, the newspaper *Media Indonesia* carried a

"I have never had illusions about the value of my individual contribution! I realized early that what a man or a woman does is built on what those who have gone before have done, that its real value depends on making the matter in hand a little clearer, a little sounder for those who come after."[3]

—*Ida Tarbell*, All in the Day's Work, 1939

story about Nike sweatshops in 1991. The story revealed that workers in the sweatshops were expected to work ten hours a day, six days a week but were paid barely half the legal minimum wage for that country.

In the 2000s, electronics factories sprang up across China. Many of these factories were owned by the Taiwanese company Foxconn, which sold parts to US brands such as Apple and Hewlett-Packard. In 2010, the Chinese investigative newspaper *Southern Weekend* reported that two Foxconn factories in China had experienced a rash of worker suicides. *Southern Weekend* reporter Liu Zhiyi had gone undercover at a Foxconn factory for 28 days, working on an assembly line. During that time, he collected information on conditions in the factory. "Some workers even envied those injured on the job because they could get days off," Liu wrote. "They joked with each other while chatting about how toxic their work was."[4] In the wake of the story, Foxconn acted quickly to improve conditions in its factories. But according to Liu, conditions at factories owned by other companies were much worse, leading him to conclude he had discovered "not an inside scoop about a factory, but the fate of an entire generation of Chinese workers."[6]

In some countries, reporters face imprisonment, injury, and even death for speaking out against the government or other powerful sectors of society. In the African nation of Angola, reporter Rafael Marques has made a career of criticizing the government at great personal risk. Marques has focused much of his attention on that nation's diamond mines. In 2005 and 2006, he published a series of reports contending government and private security groups detained, beat, tortured, and killed local residents in order to prevent illegal mining of diamonds. In one report, he describes how a woman's young son was shot

INVESTIGATIVE JOURNALISM IN COLOMBIA

Colombian reporter Tatiana Escárraga has focused attention on her country's powerful coal mining sector. In 2013, she published an article describing conditions in the remote areas where these mines are located: "Huge dumps line the road, mountains of refuse left by the coal operations. Particle emissions are so high that breathing the air has become dangerous to the health and survival of the surrounding communities."[7] Publishing such an article takes courage in a country where more than 100 journalists have been killed in the past several decades.

Angolan journalist and human rights advocate Rafael Marques has used his writing to challenge the government and some businesses in his country.

while on her back. Another man was tied up and set on fire by security guards. According to Marques, these cases were not unique:

> Like this story, there are plenty more of human beings with faces and names who get killed, tortured, maimed, or dispossessed on a daily basis in the diamond-rich region. . . . Who cares about human rights, where money, diamonds, and politicking buy or silence consciences?[8]

Marques named several senior officers of Angola's army as owners of the security companies that carried out such atrocities. As a result, few newspapers in the country were willing to print his stories for fear of retribution. So Marques began publishing them on his independent website, Maka Angola.

The Decline of Investigative Journalism

Although investigative journalism continues to be practiced today, investigative reports are not nearly as prevalent as they once were. Florence Graves of the Schuster Institute for Investigative Journalism spoke on the topic:

> *Contrary to the myth, only a skeleton crew of reporters is trying to find out how Americans' daily lives—what they*

MARQUES STANDS TRIAL

In 2011, Rafael Marques published *Blood Diamonds: Corruption and Torture in Angola.* The generals he named in his book took him to court for defamation. In 2015, a judge ruled against Marques. The judge suspended his six-month sentence for two years, which means authorities can put Marques in jail at any time during those two years.

Sarah Hager of Amnesty International US said her group would stand by Marques "to ensure his safety and freedom of movement are not impinged upon further while he continues to seek whatever justice he may find in a legal system determined to stifle his voice."[9]

The American Bar Association Center for Human Rights studied the case and noted multiple violations of international law. One was a failure to allow Marques to present a defense.

Marques refuses to be deterred by the ruling. He said, "I will continue to write, to do exactly the same things. In Africa the good guys keep leaving so that the bad guys can rule as they wish. We have to make a strong stand."[10]

eat, the medicines they take, the products they use, and the environmental conditions in which they live—are being affected by hundreds of lobbyists, dozens of . . . think-tanks, scores of federal agencies, and hundreds of officials.[11]

One reason there are not more investigative journalists today is that many magazines and newspapers have had to cut their staffs in the face of declining circulation. They often cannot afford the time and resources to allow one journalist to spend weeks, months, or even years investigating a single story. In addition, many news organizations are reluctant to cover stories that might result in lawsuits from large corporations.

NO MORE HIDDEN CAMERAS

In 1992, two producers for the ABC news show *Primetime Live* lied on job applications to secure positions at Food Lion grocery stores. With cameras hidden in their hats, the producers captured footage of employees washing expired meat in bleach and rewrapping it to be sold as fresh. In 1995, Food Lion sued ABC, saying the news network had used illegal methods to gather its information. The next year, a jury found in favor of Food Lion. The case spelled the end of hidden cameras in most investigative reporting.

Old Techniques, New Technology

Those investigative journalists who remain in the field use many of the same techniques as the first muckrakers. They rely on government documents, court records,

and firsthand accounts to
accumulate their facts,
which they then present in
an engaging narrative that
draws readers' interest.
Today's journalists have
an advantage over the
muckrakers of the early
1900s. Technology
such as the Internet
has made it possible for
journalists to find large
volumes of information
almost instantaneously.

The Internet has
also extended the reach
of investigative reports
because it connects people
around the world. This has
led to the development of what Dan Gillmor, director of
the Knight Center for Digital Media Entrepreneurship,
calls "citizen media."[12] This is the ability of people
everywhere—whether professional journalists or not—
to create, publish, and comment on the news. Gillmor
believes ordinary citizens "have made huge contributions

NONPROFIT NEWS

In the wake of declining investigative work in the traditional media, several nonprofit media groups have been formed. Among them are ProPublica, the Center for Public Integrity, the Pulitzer Center on Crisis Reporting, and the Center for Investigative Reporting. These organizations specialize in investigative journalism, which they publish online or provide to traditional news outlets. They stress that they are independent, with no partisan or ideological agenda. The goal of these nonprofit groups is much the same as that of the early muckrakers—to expose corruption and to inspire the public to act.

Technology allows immediate reporting. Anti-government protesters used a tablet to record a police line at a large rally in Bangkok, Thailand, in 2013.

to the coverage of world events" such as the 2004 tsunami that devastated Southeast Asia.[13]

Citizen media brings challenges as well. With so many people posting so many things online every day, it can be hard to evaluate the information to "sort the good from the bad, the useful from the trivial and, crucially, the trustworthy from the phony," according to Gillmor.[14] In fact, the Internet has made it easy to publish untrustworthy and downright false information. Gillmor stresses how important it is for anyone who publishes news to learn the journalistic principles of fairness, accuracy, and thoroughness.

These are the very principles first established by Ida Tarbell and the muckrakers. In their day, the fight was against big business, government corruption, and inequality. A century later, today's fights are not so different. Tarbell and the muckrakers blazed the trail for today's investigative journalists. Perhaps most important, they served as examples of how one person can expose injustice and, in exposing it, help correct it.

TIMELINE

1857
Ida Tarbell is born on November 5.

1883
Joseph Pulitzer buys the *New York World*.

1887
Reporter Nellie Bly reports on an undercover investigation of an insane asylum.

1893
In June, Samuel S. McClure publishes the first issue of *McClure's Magazine*.

1894
Tarbell accepts a position on the staff of *McClure's*.

1895
William Randolph Hearst purchases the *New York Morning Journal* and begins a circulation war with the *World*, leading to yellow journalism.

1901
Theodore Roosevelt becomes president after the assassination of William McKinley.

1902
McClure's publishes the first article in Tarbell's Standard Oil series in November.

1903
The January issue of *McClure's* contains three investigative articles and marks the start of the muckraking era; the US Congress forms the Department of Commerce and Labor and passes stronger antitrust laws.

1904
Upton Sinclair investigates meatpacking plants in Chicago, Illinois, for a series published as the book *The Jungle* in 1906.

1906
On April 14, Roosevelt delivers a public speech in which he coins the term *muckrakers* for investigative journalists; Tarbell and several other muckraking journalists leave *McClure's* and purchase *American Magazine*.

1911

On May 15, the US Supreme Court orders Standard Oil to sell 33 subsidiaries.

1914

World War I draws the public's attention, and the muckraking era comes to an end.

1939

John Steinbeck's *The Grapes of Wrath* is published, exposing the difficult conditions faced by migrant farmers.

1954

Edward R. Murrow's *See It Now* broadcasts a series about communist-hunting Senator Joseph McCarthy.

1972

Washington Post reporters Bob Woodward and Carl Bernstein investigate the Watergate scandal.

2001

Eric Schlosser discusses the modern meatpacking industry in his book *Fast Food Nation*.

2004

The Abu Ghraib prisoner abuse scandal is uncovered by *60 Minutes II* and Seymour Hersh, writing for the *New Yorker*.

2010

The Chinese newspaper *Southern Weekend* reports on conditions in electronics sweatshops, which have experienced a rash of suicides.

ESSENTIAL FACTS

KEY FIGURES

- Ida Tarbell was one of the first muckrakers. She exposed the corrupt methods used by the Standard Oil Company to achieve a monopoly in the oil industry. Her work led to the establishment of new antitrust legislation and the dissolution of Standard Oil.

- Samuel S. McClure founded *McClure's* as an inexpensive magazine for the middle class. By championing articles exposing corruption, he helped bring about the muckraking era.

- Lincoln Steffens was an early muckraker who focused much of his energy at *McClure's* on corruption in city governments.

- As a *McClure's* reporter, Ray Stannard Baker helped call attention to the plight of the working class. Later, he focused on racial inequalities.

- Upton Sinclair used his fictional work *The Jungle* to highlight ghastly working conditions in Chicago's meatpacking district.

- President Theodore Roosevelt worked closely with the muckrakers to spread his message of reform. Their articles, in turn, helped him to pass his reform agenda through Congress.

KEY WORKS

- The History of the Standard Oil Company was Tarbell's 19-part series about the Standard Oil Company that led to legislative reforms and the forced breakup of the Standard Oil Trust.

- The Shame of the Cities series included articles by Steffens about cities from Saint Louis to Minneapolis. Articles revealed fraud in government and helped bring about the defeat of corrupt officials.

- *The Jungle*, by Sinclair, aimed to call attention to the plight of workers, but the novel instead sparked a cry for reform of the nation's food safety laws.

- The Treason of the Senate was a series in which David Graham Phillips called out corrupt senators. This angered Roosevelt, leading the president to give investigative journalists the name *muckrakers*. But the series also led to changes in the way senators were elected.

IMPACT ON SOCIETY

The muckrakers helped call attention to problems in society. Their coverage helped the Progressive movement by sparking public outcry and calls for reform. As a result of muckraking articles, new laws were established to limit the power of trusts, end child labor, and regulate food safety. The muckrakers also established investigative journalism, which continues to be practiced today.

QUOTE

"And what are we going to do about it? For it is *our* business. We the people of the United States and nobody else must cure whatever is wrong in the industrial situation, typified by this narrative of the growth of the Standard Oil Company."

—*Ida Tarbell, in the final article in her series about Standard Oil*

GLOSSARY

ANARCHIST
A person who believes countries should not have governments.

BYLINE
A line naming the author of an article in a newspaper or magazine.

CENSURE
To strongly criticize.

COMMUNIST
A person who believes in communism, an economic system based on the elimination of private ownership of factories, land, and other means of economic production.

DEFAMATION
The act of damaging someone's reputation through false statements.

DERRICK
A structure built over an oil well that holds and guides the tool used to dig the well and get the oil.

EDITORIAL
An opinion essay by the editor of a publication.

EXPOSÉ
An exposure or revelation of something discreditable.

GENOCIDE
The deliberate mass murder of a group of people.

LYNCHING

The act of illegally killing a person through mob action.

MONEY LAUNDERING

Hiding the true source of income as from criminal activity by using a front, such as an actual business.

MONOPOLY

Exclusive control over a commodity or service.

REFINERY

A factory where oil or another substance is refined, or purified.

SEGREGATION

The practice of separating groups of people based on race, gender, ethnicity, or other factors.

SOCIALISM

A political and economic theory that advocates resources and property being shared equally among members of society.

SUBSIDIARY

A company owned by another company.

SYNDICATE

An organization that sells content to many newspapers or other media outlets.

TENEMENT

A large apartment building usually located in a poor area of a city.

ADDITIONAL
RESOURCES

SELECTED BIBLIOGRAPHY

Schiffrin, Anya, ed. *Global Muckraking: 100 Years of Investigative Journalism from around the World.* New York: New Press, 2014. Print.

Serrin, Judith, and William Serrin, eds. *Muckraking! The Journalism That Changed America.* New York: New Press, 2002. Print.

Weinberg, Steve. *Taking on the Trust: The Epic Battle of Ida Tarbell and John D. Rockefeller.* New York: Norton, 2008. Print.

FURTHER READINGS

Gitlin, Martin. *Joseph Pulitzer: Historic Newspaper Publisher.* Minneapolis: Abdo, 2009. Print.

Goldsmith, Bonnie. *William Randolph Hearst: Newspaper Magnate.* Minneapolis: Abdo, 2009. Print.

McCully, Emily Arnold. *Ida M. Tarbell: The Woman Who Challenged Big Business—and Won!* New York: Carlion, 2014. Print.

WEBSITES

To learn more about Hidden Heroes, visit **booklinks.abdopublishing.com**. These links are routinely monitored and updated to provide the most current information available.

FOR MORE INFORMATION

For more information on this subject, contact or visit the following organizations:

ALLEGHENY COLLEGE
520 North Main Street
Meadville, PA 16335
814-332-3789
http://sites.allegheny.edu/tarbell/
Pelletier Library on the Allegheny College Campus houses the Ida M. Tarbell collection, which includes Tarbell's research materials, letters, and notes, along with photographs and other items from Tarbell's life.

NATIONAL WOMEN'S HALL OF FAME
76 Fall Street
Seneca Falls, NY 13148
315-568-8060
https://www.womenofthehall.org/
Despite her antisuffrage views, in 2000, Tarbell was inducted into the National Women's Hall of Fame, honoring her as a role model for both men and women journalists.

NEWSEUM
555 Pennsylvania Avenue NW
Washington, DC 20001
202-292-6100
http://www.newseum.org/
Opened in 2008, the Newseum contains seven levels of interactive exhibits highlighting important developments in journalism as well as the coverage of newsworthy events throughout history.

SOURCE NOTES

CHAPTER 1. SEEDS OF CONFLICT

1. Ida M. Tarbell. *All in the Day's Work.* New York: Macmillan, 1939. Print. 206.
2. David Copeland. *The Media's Role in Defining the Nation.* New York: Peter Lang, 2010. 133. *Google Books.* Web. 13 Sept. 2016.
3. Ron Chernow. *Titan: The Life of John D. Rockefeller, Sr.* New York: Random, 1998. Print. 443.
4. Ida M. Tarbell. *All in the Day's Work.* New York: Macmillan, 1939. Print. 5.
5. Ibid. 9.
6. Kevin Hillstrom and Laurie Collier Hillstrom, eds. *Industrial Revolution in America.* Santa Barbara, CA: ABC-CLIO, 108. *Google Books.* Web. 13 Sept. 2016.
7. Ida M. Tarbell. *All in the Day's Work.* New York: Macmillan, 1939. Print. 23–24.
8. Ibid. 26.
9. Ibid. 203.

CHAPTER 2. KEEPING THE PEOPLE INFORMED

1. Joseph Turow. *Media Today: An Introduction to Mass Communication.* 4th ed. New York: Routledge, 2011. Print. 261.
2. "New York Sun." *Encyclopædia Britannica.* Encyclopædia Britannica, 2016. Web. 13 Sept. 2016.
3. "The Great Moon Hoax." *History.* A+E Television, 2016. Web. 13 Sept. 2016.
4. Joseph Pulitzer. "Editorial." *World.* 11 May 1883. *Columbia University Libraries.* Web. 13 Sept. 2016.
5. Judith and William Serrin, eds. *Muckraking!* New York: New, 2002. Print. 146.
6. Alleyne Ireland. *Joseph Pulitzer.* New York: Mitchell Kennerley, 1914. Print. 115.
7. Helen MacGill Hughes. *News and the Human Interest Story.* New Brunswick, NJ: Transaction, 2014. Print. 205.
8. Doris Kearns Goodwin. *The Bully Pulpit.* New York: Simon, 2013. Print. 204.
9. Jacob Riis. *How the Other Half Lives.* New York: Scribner's, 1914. Print. 3.
10. Alfreda M. Duster, ed. *Crusade for Justice.* Chicago: U of Chicago P, 1970. Print. 24.
11. Ibid. 64.
12. Ida B. Wells. "Editorial." *Muckraking!* Eds. Judith and William Serrin. New York: New, 2002. Print. 179.
13. "National Assessment of Adult Literacy." *National Center for Education Statistics.* National Center for Education Statistics, n.d. Web. 13 Sept. 2016.
14. Anastacia Kurylo, ed. *Intercultural Communication.* Los Angeles: Sage, 2013. 238. *Google Books.* Web. 13 Sept. 2016.

CHAPTER 3. A MAGAZINE FOR EVERYONE

1. Ida M. Tarbell. "The Arts and Industries of Cincinnati." *Chautauquan* VII (Oct. 1886–July 1887): 162. *Google Books.* Web. 13 Sept. 2016.
2. Ida M. Tarbell. *All in the Day's Work.* New York: Macmillan, 1939. Print. 80.
3. Samuel Sidney McClure and Willa Cather. *My Autobiography.* New York: Stokes, 1914. 218. *Google Books.* Web. 13 Sept. 2016.
4. Doris Kearns Goodwin. *The Bully Pulpit.* New York: Simon, 2013. Print. 333.
5. Ibid. 170.
6. Ibid. 169.
7. Ibid.

8. Steve Weinberg. *Taking on the Trust*. New York: Norton, 2008. Print. 176.

9. *American Journalism* 6 (1989): 9. *Google Books*. Web. 13 Sept. 2016.

10. Doris Kearns Goodwin. *The Bully Pulpit*. New York: Simon, 2013. Print. 225, 227.

11. Ida M. Tarbell. *All in the Day's Work*. New York: Macmillan, 1939. Print. 196.

CHAPTER 4. THE STANDARD OIL COMPANY

1. Michael McGerr. *A Fierce Discontent*. New York: Free, 2003. Print. 15.

2. Ida M. Tarbell. *All in the Day's Work*. New York: Macmillan, 1939. Print. 204.

3. Paul S. Boyer, ed. *The Oxford Companion to United States History*. New York: Oxford UP, 2001. 206. *Google Books*. Web. 13 Sept. 2016.

4. "John D. Rockefeller." *History*. A+E Television, 2016. Web. 13 Sept. 2016.

5. Doris Kearns Goodwin. *The Bully Pulpit*. New York: Simon, 2013. Print. 334.

6. Ida M. Tarbell. *All in the Day's Work*. New York: Macmillan, 1939. Print. 212.

7. Ida M. Tarbell. "John D. Rockefeller: A Character Study, Part Two." *McClure's Magazine*, August 1905. 386. *UNZ.org*. Web. 13 Sept. 2016.

8. Ida M. Tarbell. "The Birth of an Industry." *McClure's Magazine* (November 1902): 16. *UNZ.org*. Web. 13 Sept. 2016.

9. Ida M. Tarbell. "The Great Consummation." *McClure's Magazine* (June 1903): 215. *UNZ.org*. Web. 13 Sept. 2016.

10. Ibid.

11. Ida M. Tarbell. "Conclusion." *McClure's Magazine* (October 1904): 671. *UNZ.org*. Web.

12. Ida M. Tarbell. *All in the Day's Work*. New York: Macmillan, 1939. Print. 195.

13. Steve Weinberg. *Taking on the Trust*. New York: Norton, 2008. Print. 225.

14. Robert Kochersberger, ed. *More Than a Muckraker*. Knoxville: U of Tennessee P, 1994. Print. 66.

15. Steve Weinberg. "Taking on the Trust." *Wall Street Journal*. Dow Jones, 27 Mar. 2008. Web. 13 Sept. 2016.

16. Doris Kearns Goodwin. *The Bully Pulpit*. New York: Simon, 2013. Print. 339.

17. Ibid. 339.

18. Ibid. 339.

CHAPTER 5. DAWN OF THE MUCKRAKERS

1. Samuel McClure. "Editorial." *McClure's Magazine* (January 1903): 336. *UNZ.org*. Web. 13 Sept. 2016.

2. Ibid.

3. Ida M. Tarbell. *All in the Day's Work*. New York: Macmillan, 1939. Print. 199.

4. Doris Kearns Goodwin. *The Bully Pulpit*. New York: Simon, 2013. Print. 180.

5. Robert C. Kochersberger Jr., ed. *More Than a Muckraker*. Knoxville: U of Tennessee P, 1994. Print. xxv.

6. *Revue Française D'études Américaines*. 1978. 176. *Google Books*. Web. 13 Sept. 2016.

7. Upton Sinclair. *The Autobiography of Upton Sinclair*. New York: Harcourt, 1962. Print. 109.

8. Upton Sinclair. *The Jungle*. 1906. New York: Bantam, 1981. Print. 129.

9. Ibid. 135.

10. "N. W. Ayer and Son's American Newspaper Annual." *Library of Congress*, Library of Congress, n.d. Web. 13 Sept. 2016.

SOURCE NOTES
CONTINUED

11. Bruce Jennings and David Callahan, eds. *Representation and Responsibility*. New York: Plenum, 1985. 18. *Google Books*. Web. 13 Sept. 2016.

12. David Graham Phillips. "New York's Misrepresentatives." *Muckraking!* Eds. Judith and William Serrin. New York: New, 2002. Print. 106.

13. Judith and William Serrin, eds. *Muckraking!* New York: New, 2002. Print. 310.

14. Edward Bok. "The 'Patent-Medicine' Curse." *Muckraking!* Eds. Judith and William Serrin. New York: New, 2002. Print. 310.

15. John Spargo. *The Bitter Cry of the Children*. New York: Macmillan, 1906. 164. *Google Books*. Web. 13 Sept. 2016.

16. Judith and William Serrin, eds. *Muckraking!* New York: New, 2002. Print. xx.

CHAPTER 6. THE PROGRESSIVE ERA

1. Michael McGerr. *A Fierce Discontent*. New York: Free, 2003. Print. xiii.

2. Doris Kearns Goodwin. *The Bully Pulpit*. New York: Simon, 2013. Print. 341.

3. Richard Hofstadter and Beatrice K. Hofstadter, eds. *Great Issues in American History*. New York: Vintage, 1982. 250. *Google Books*. Web. 13 Sept. 2016.

4. David A. Copeland. *The Media's Role in Defining the Nation*. New York: Peter Lang, 210. 133. *Google Books*. Web. 13 Sept. 2016.

5. Theodore Roosevelt. "First Annual Message: December 3, 1901." *The American Presidency Project*. Regents of the University of California, 2016. Web. 13 Sept. 2016.

6. Jessica Dorman. "Where Are Muckraking Journalists Today?" *Nieman Reports*. Presidents and Fellows of Harvard College, 15 June 2000. Web. 13 Sept. 2016.

7. Judith and William Serrin, eds. *Muckraking!* New York: New, 2002. Print. xx.

8. Doris Kearns Goodwin. *The Bully Pulpit*. New York: Simon, 2013. Print. 347.

9. Ray Stannard Baker. *Following the Color Line*. New York: Doubleday, 1908. Print. 120.

10. "Upton Sinclair's *The Jungle*." Constitutional Rights Foundation. Bill of Rights Foundation, fall 2008. Web. 13 Sept. 2016.

CHAPTER 7. END OF THE MUCKRAKERS

1. Harold S. Wilson. *McClure's Magazine and the Muckrakers*. Princeton, NJ: Princeton UP, 1970. 179. *Google Books*. Web. 13 Sept. 2016.

2. Doris Kearns Goodwin. *The Bully Pulpit*. New York: Simon, 2013. Print. 482.

3. Ibid. 483.

4. Ibid. 485.

5. Ibid.

6. Theodore Roosevelt. "Address of President Roosevelt at the Laying of the Corner Stone of the Office Building of the House of Representatives (The Man with the Muck-Rake) (14 April 1906)." *Voices of Democracy*. Voice of Democracy, n.d. Web. 13 Sept. 2016.

7. Ibid.

8. Ida M. Tarbell. *All in the Day's Work*. New York: Macmillan, 1939. Print. 242.

9. Ibid. 241.

10. Ellen Fitzpatrick, ed. *Muckraking*. Boston: Bedford, 1994. Print. 114.

11. Doris Kearns Goodwin. *The Bully Pulpit*. New York: Simon, 2013. Print. 491.

12. Ibid. 487.

13. Ibid. 491.

14. Ida M. Tarbell. *All in the Day's Work*. New York: Macmillan, 1939. Print. 195.

CHAPTER 8. RESURGENCE

1. Judith and William Serrin, eds. *Muckraking!* New York: New, 2002. Print. 11.
2. Ibid. 284.
3. William G. Rothstein. *Public Health and the Risk Factor.* Rochester, NY: University of Rochester Press, 2003. 257. *Google Books.* Web. 13 Sept. 2016.
4. Roy Norr. "Cancer by the Carton." *Muckraking!* Eds. Judith and William Serrin. New York: New, 2002. Print. 54–55.
5. "Current Cigarette Smoking Among Adults in the United States." *Centers for Disease Control and Prevention.* US Department of Health and Human Services, 14 Mar. 2016. Web. 13 Sept. 2016.
6. David Shedden. "Edward R. Murrow Investigated Joe McCarthy on 'See It Now.'" *Poynter.* Poynter Institute, 9 Mar. 2015. Web. 13 Sept. 2016.
7. "Vietnam War." *Encyclopædia Britannica.* Encyclopædia Britannica, 2016. Web. 13 Sept. 2016.
8. Judith and William Serrin, eds. *Muckraking!* New York: New, 2002. Print. 294.
9. Ibid.
10. John Howard Griffin. "Black Like Me." *Muckraking!* Eds. Judith and William Serrin. New York: New, 2002. Print. 194.
11. Judith and William Serrin, eds. *Muckraking!* New York: New, 2002. Print. 294.
12. "Watergate Scandal." *Encyclopædia Britannica.* Encyclopædia Britannica, 2016. Web. 13 Sept. 2016.
13. Judith and William Serrin, eds. *Muckraking!* New York: New, 2002. Print. 388

CHAPTER 9. LEGACY OF TRUTH

1. Seymour M. Hersh. "Torture at Abu Ghraib." *New Yorker.* Condé Nast, 10 May 2004. Web. 13 Sept. 2016.
2. Dana Priest. "Soldiers Face Neglect, Frustration at Army's Top Medical Facility." *Washington Post.* Washington Post, 18 Feb. 2007. Web. 13 Sept. 2016.
3. Ida M. Tarbell. *All in the Day's Work.* New York: Macmillan, 1939. Print. 400.
4. Liu Zhiyi. "Youth and Destiny Spent with Machines—28 Days Undercover at Foxconn." *Global Muckraking.* Ed. Anya Schiffrin. New York: New, 2013. Print. 57.
5. Marisa Guthrie. "Investigative Journalism Under Fire." *Broadcasting & Cable.* NewBay Media, 22 June 2008. Web. 13 Sept. 2016.
6. Liu Zhiyi. "Youth and Destiny Spent with Machines—28 Days Undercover at Foxconn." *Global Muckraking.* Ed. Anya Schiffrin. New York: New, 2013. Print. 58.
7. Tatiana Escárraga. "Villages Swallowed by Coal." *Global Muckraking.* Ed. Anya Schiffrin. New York: New, 2013. Print. 150.
8. Rafael Marques. "The Tale of a Brave Woman." *Global Muckraking.* Ed. Anya Schiffrin. New York: New, 2013. Print. 132.
9. Kerry A. Dolan. "Journalist Rafael Marques Given Two-Year Suspended Sentence in Angolan Defamation Trial." *Forbes.* Forbes, 28 May 2015. Web. 13 Sept. 2016.
10. Ibid.
11. Florence Graves. "Watchdog Reporting." *Nieman Reports.* President and Fellows if Harvard College, 15 Mar. 2008. Web. 13 Sept. 2016.
12. Dan Gillmor. "Bloggers and Mash." *New Scientist,* 15 Mar. 2008. *EBSCO MasterFile Premier.* Web. 13 Sept. 2016.
13. Ibid.
14. Ibid.

INDEX

ABOUT THE
AUTHOR

Valerie Bodden has written more than 200 nonfiction books for children. Her books have received positive reviews from *School Library Journal, Booklist, Children's Literature, ForeWord Magazine, Horn Book Guide, VOYA,* and *Library Media Connection.* Valerie lives in Wisconsin with her husband and four young children.